Copyright © 2016 by Kandra Albury

All rights reserved. No part of this publication may be reproduced, distributed, or transmitted in any form or by any means, including photocopying, recording, or other electronic or mechanical methods, without the prior written permission of the publisher, except in the case of brief quotations embodied in critical reviews and certain other noncommercial uses permitted by copyright law.

Books may be order through online retailers or by contacting:

Kandra Albury
www.kandraalbury.org

Illustrated by Jamie Cosley
www.jamiecosley.com

ISBN: 978-0-692-91465-6

Children's Fiction/Fiction

# MEET THE FEISTY FOUR!!

**Sassy Simone**
Age: 5 ½ (birthday July 29th)
Grade: Kindergarten
Favorite subject: Spelling
Favorite food: Macaroni and cheese
Favorite color: Green
Hobbies: Trying on her mommy's earrings, playing with her dog Oreo and her friend Karate-chop Kimmy

**Karate-chop Kimmy**
Age: 7 (birthday February 19th)
Grade: Second
Favorite subject: Reading
Favorite food: Spaghetti and meatballs
Favorite color: Red
Hobbies: Playing dress up with her friend Sassy Simone and practicing her karate moves

# MEET THE FEISTY FOUR!!

**Courageous Cody**
Age: 6 (birthday August 25th)
Grade: First
Favorite subject: Math
Favorite food: Pizza
Favorite color: Orange
Hobbies: Playing with his cat Cotton and his friend Daring Diego

**Daring Diego**
Age: 7 (birthday September 6th)
Grade: Second
Favorite subject: Science
Favorite food: Peanut butter and jelly sandwich (crust removed)
Favorite color: Blue
Hobbies: Looking for bugs outside and playing with his friend Courageous Cody

WE ARE THE FEISTY FOUR AND WE WON'T BE BULLIED ANYMORE!

YES, WE HAVE EACH OTHER'S BACKS; WE DON'T PUT UP WITH TEASING OR ATTACKS!

I'M SASSY SIMONE! THINKING ABOUT BULLYING ME? YOU BETTER LEAVE ME ALONE!

I FLOAT LIKE A BUTTERFLY AND STING LIKE A BEE.....
AND I WON'T ALLOW YOU TO PICK ON ME!

DON'T MAKE FUN OF MY SKIN COLOR, CLOTHES AND HAIR. BULLYING IS NOT NICE, IT'S JUST NOT FAIR!

SO WHAT IF I WEAR BRACES AND GLASSES, I NEED TO SEE TO MAKE As IN MY CLASSES!

12

CALL ME NAMES...
I WON'T BACK DOWN!
YOU CAN'T TURN THIS
SMILE INTO A FROWN.

PICKING ON PEOPLE WHO ARE SMALLER THAN YOU...BET YOU'D RUN IF I SAID BOO!

15

I WON'T BE BULLIED ON THE BUS OR AT SCHOOL. BULLYING ANYWHERE IS JUST NOT COOL!

EXCUSE ME, CAN'T YOU SEE THIS IS A NO-BULLYING ZONE? SO GO OVER THERE AND LEAVE US ALONE!

THERE'S NOTHING COOL ABOUT BEING A BULLY. TRUTH BE TOLD, YOU JUST LOOK SILLY!

22

...GOING AROUND PICKING ON PEOPLE WHO ARE WEAK, I STAND UP FOR MYSELF EVERY DAY OF THE WEEK!

THINK I WON'T TELL?
WELL TELLING IS WHAT I'LL
DO, ESPECIALLY IF A BULLY
TRIES TO PICK ON ME
AND YOU!

I GO TO SCHOOL TO LEARN, HAVE FUN AND FEEL SAFE. SO DON'T YOU DARE GET IN MY FACE!

BULLYING STOPS RIGHT HERE, RIGHT NOW - TODAY! ALL YOU HAVE TO SAY IS, "HEY GO AWAY!"

BEING BULLIED IS NEVER OK SO FIND SOME COURAGE TO FACE YOUR BULLY TODAY.

YOU CAN DO IT!
JUST BE STRONG.
YOU NEVER HAVE TO
FACE YOUR BULLY
ALONE!

Tell your mom, dad and teachers too! I want you to be safe because I care about you!

36

YES, I WILL STAND UP FOR MYSELF AND OTHERS TOO AND NOT TOLERATE BULLYING FROM MEAN'OLE YOU!

38

# Dedication

I dedicate this book to all kid-sized superheroes around the globe. My mission is to give boys and girls the courage to discover and activate their superpower–courage–immediately when they feel threatened or unsafe. Remember, it's your right to always feel safe.

Special thank you to my husband James, my children, family and friends for their support; you all are the wind beneath my cape.

Jamie Cosley, you are the best illustrator ever. Thank you for courageously and creatively bringing the Feisty Four characters to life!

I am confident that children will be empowered to courageously take a stand against bullying and immediately tell an adult to ensure their safety as well as the safety of their family and friends.

Courageously yours,

Kandra

## Five Anti-bullying Tips for Everyday Kid-sized Superheroes:

1). Be courageous enough to stand up to your bullies. Calmly tell them to stop it, then turn and walk away.

2). Tell a parent/guardian or another responsible adult. It is your right to feel safe no matter where you are. Remember, you're not snitching or being a tattletale when it comes to your personal safety or the safety of others.

3). Don't be a bystander, be a friend to the person who is being bullied. Help them to speak up for themselves.

4). Think safety first and avoid places where bullies hang out. Always walk with a friend or with a group of people. There's safety in numbers.

5). Apologize if you have bullied someone or said mean things. An apology helps everyone to feel better.

## The Promise to Tell and Listen Agreement

I (child's name) _____ promise to immediately tell an adult when someone is bullying me.

I/we (the adult) _____ promise to always listen and take immediate action when a child tells me that someone is bullying him/her.

Today's date_____

Draw a picture of yourself in a courageous superhero pose!
(Don't forget your cape!)

Make sure you share your drawing on the Kids'N Capes Facebook page!
**facebook.com/CourageIsTheNewSuperpower/**

# FEISTY FOUR COLORING SHEET
## COURAGEOUS CODY

For additional printable coloring sheets, visit **kandraalbury.org/just-4-kids**

# FEISTY FOUR COLORING SHEET
## DARING DIEGO

For additional printable coloring sheets, visit **kandraalbury.org/just-4-kids**

# FEISTY FOUR COLORING SHEET
## SASSY SIMONE

For additional printable coloring sheets, visit **kandraalbury.org/just-4-kids**

# FEISTY FOUR COLORING SHEET
## KARATE CHOP KIMMY

For additional printable coloring sheets, visit **kandraalbury.org/just-4-kids**

# FEISTY FOUR COLORING SHEET
## MEET THE FEISTY 4

For additional printable coloring sheets, visit **kandraalbury.org/just-4-kids**

www.ingramcontent.com/pod-product-compliance
Lightning Source LLC
Chambersburg PA
CBHW042139290426
44110CB00002B/66